NATURE CLOSE-UP

SNAILS *and* SLUGS

TEXT BY ELAINE PASCOE

PHOTOGRAPHS BY DWIGHT KUHN

BLACKBIRCH PRESS INC.

WOODBRIDGE, CO1

Published by Blackbirch Press, Inc.
260 Amity Road
Woodbridge, CT 06525

©1999 by Blackbirch Press, Inc.
Text ©1999 by Elaine Pascoe
Photographs ©1999 by Dwight Kuhn
First Edition

Email: staff@blackbirch.com
Web site: www.blackbirch.com

Printed in the United States

10 9 8 7 6 5 4 3 2 1

For Brandie	To S.M.S.
–D.K.	–E.P.

front cover: West Coast land snail
back cover: (left to right) West Coast land snail laying eggs, snail eggs hatching, land snails eating leaf, adult land snail

Library of Congress Cataloging-in-Publication Data

Pascoe, Elaine.
Snails and slugs / by Elaine Pascoe. — 1st ed.
  p.   cm. — (Nature close-up)
  Includes bibliographical references (p. 47) and index.
  Summary: Describes the physical characteristics, reproduction processes, habitats, and meta-morphoses of snails and slugs and provides instructions for related hands-on science projects.
  ISBN 1-56711-181-5 (lib. bdg. : alk. paper)
  1. Snails—Juvenile literature. 2. Slugs (Mollusks)—Juvenile literature. [1. Snails. 2. Slugs (Mollusks). 3. Snails—Experiments. 4. Slugs (Mollusks)—Experiments. 5. Experiments.] I. Title. II. Series: Pascoe, Elaine. Nature close-up.
  QL430.4.P285   1999
  594'.3—dc21
                                                                                    97-29159
                                                                                    CIP
                                                                                    AC

Note on metric conversions: The metric conversions given in Chapters 2 and 3 of this book are not always exact equivalents of U.S. measures. Instead, they provide a workable quantity for each experiment in metric units. The abbreviations used are:

cm	centimeter	**kg**	kilogram
m	meter	**l**	liter
g	gram	**cc**	cubic centimeter

CONTENTS

1 Slow and Slimy   **4**

    Shell Games   6

    Ugh—Slime!   8

    Life at a Snail's Pace   11

    Snails, Slugs, and People   18

2 Collecting and Caring for Snails and Slugs   **20**

    Land Snails and Slugs   24

    Caring for Land Snails   25

    Freshwater Snails   28

    Caring for Freshwater Snails   30

3 Investigating Snails and Slugs   **32**

    What Do Land Snails and Slugs Like to Eat?   32

    How Much Do Snails and Slugs Eat?   34

    Can Freshwater Snails Control Algae Growth?   36

    How Does Cold Affect the Eggs of Freshwater Snails? 37

    Do Snails Prefer Dark or Light Places?   39

    More Activities with Snails and Slugs   40

    Results and Conclusions   43

Some Words About Snails and Slugs   **46**

Sources for Snails   **46**

For Further Reading   **47**

Index   **47**

1

Slow and Slimy

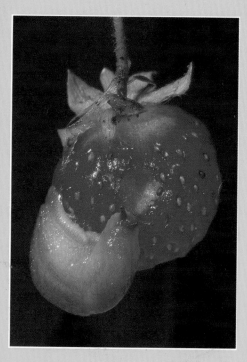

A thin, silvery trail across a stone, a few holes nibbled in tender leaves—these are signs that snails have paid a visit to your garden. Snails and their shell-less relatives, slugs, are found all over the world. But you often have to look closely to find them.

There are more than 80,000 different kinds of snails and slugs worldwide. They range in size from tiny creatures—hardly bigger than the period at the end of this sentence—to giants more than a foot (30 centimeters) long. Snails live on land, in fresh water, and in the ocean. Sea slugs (called nudibranchs) live in the ocean, while all other slugs are terrestrial, or live on land. Snails and slugs can be found in all sorts of climates, from tropical jungles to cold northern forests.

Many people don't like snails and slugs because they are slimy—especially slugs. Gardeners and farmers view these animals as pests because garden slugs and snails eat plants. But snails and slugs hold an important place in nature, providing food for larger animals (including people). And they are fascinating to watch.

5

SHELL GAMES

Snails can be divided into three groups depending on where they live: in the ocean, in freshwater, or on land. Similarly, slugs can be divided into two groups, land or ocean. There are similarities among the groups, but also many differences. For example, sea snails and nudibranchs take in oxygen from the water through gills, while those that live on land have lungs and breathe air. Many freshwater snails also have lungs, and have to come to the surface to breathe. All snails and slugs are mollusks, members of a large family of animals that have existed on Earth for hundreds of millions of years. Oysters and octopuses are also members of this family.

All slugs and snails are members of the mollusk family. Various kinds of snails include the Periwinkle (above) the Ramshorn water snail (below left) and the mystery snail (below right).

Above: Slugs do not have shells. *Below:* A snail's shell is formed mainly by calcium that is secreted by the animal.

Like all mollusks, snails and slugs do not have bony skeletons. Instead, snails have hard shells. A snail shell is always a single spiral, but each species has its own shell style. There are shells shaped like cones, turbans, pointed spires, and flat cinnamon rolls. Some shells spiral right to left, and some left to right. The shells of most land and freshwater snails are drab and dull, but tropical tree snails and many sea snails have shells with bright colors and patterns. A snail shell is made of protein and minerals, mainly calcium, which the snail secretes.

7

FIXING UP THE HOUSE

As a snail grows, its shell grows with it. Nearly all snails add new shell material at the open end, making an ever-larger spiral. Cowries and olive snails—sea snails that live in tropical waters—have a different method. When a cowry or olive snail crawls along the sea floor, it covers its shell completely with the part of its soft body called the mantle. Through the mantle, it secretes new material to enlarge the shell. The mantle also spruces up the exterior, adding fresh color and giving the surface a high polish. Collectors love to find cowry and olive shells because they are unusual and beautiful.

A snail carries its shell on its back most of the time. When it's threatened, however, it can pull its whole body inside. Some snails, including most sea snails, can even slam the door against danger—they have a hard, flat plate, called an operculum, which fits over the opening when the animal is safely inside.

A slug's body is covered on top only by a mantle—a layer of soft tissue. When the slug is threatened, it tries to shrink up under its mantle, but the mantle doesn't offer much protection. Land slugs, like land snails, are mostly drab. Nudibranchs (sea slugs), that live in tropical waters often have bold colors and patterns.

UGH—SLIME!

Snails and slugs seem to creep along on their bellies. But what looks like the animal's belly is actually its broad, flat foot. (Snails and slugs are classed as gastropods, a term that comes from Latin words meaning "stomach foot.") The muscular foot pushes the animal forward with wave-like contractions. On land, snails and slugs secrete mucus as they glide forward to make the path slippery and for protection from debris and rough spots. That is why they're famous for their slime. Progress is slow, though. Three inches (8 centimeters) a minute is pretty fast for most slugs!

Compared to its foot, a snail's head is tiny—just big enough for a mouth and two or four tentacles. The mouth is on the underside, just in front of the foot. Snails and slugs breathe through a hole located farther back on the body, at the edge of the mantle.

Sea snails usually have one pair of tentacles, or feelers, with an eye at the base of each. Land snails and slugs, and some freshwater snails, have two pairs of tentacles: a short set near the mouth, and a longer set above them. The snail's eyes are at the tips of these long tentacles. The snail raises the tentacles to peer around, and retracts them quickly when it is threatened.

From the underside, you can see a snail's mouth—the opening up near the tentacles.

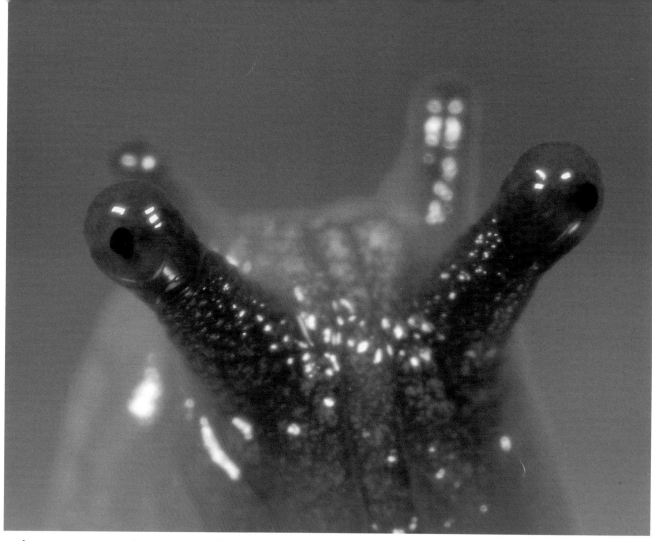

A slug's eyes peer out from the tips of its tentacles.

Snails and slugs don't have much in the way of brains—just a pair of nerve centers located behind their tentacles. That's enough to help these animals accomplish their most important tasks: finding food and mates.

KILLER SNAILS!

One family of sea snails includes some deadly members. Cone snails, which live mainly near coral reefs in the South Pacific and Indian oceans, eat small fish and other animals. They have poisonous stingers, which they use to stun their prey. The venom, or poison, of some cone snails is so powerful that people stung by these creatures have died.

Cone snails don't attack people—but they will sting if they are disturbed. Divers are always warned to avoid them. Medical researchers are studying cone snail venom, however, which may become a source for new painkillers or other medications.

LIFE AT A SNAIL'S PACE

Snails and slugs spend most of their time creeping around in search of food. Land and freshwater snails are mainly plant eaters. Some species are especially fond of tender leaves and shoots and juicy vegetables and berries, which annoys gardeners. But many snails and slugs eat dead plants and animals. They are part of the natural clean-up team that recycles decaying material. Snails and slugs have a file-like organ, called a radula, in their mouths. The radula is covered with fine teeth, and the animal uses it to rasp off particles of food.

Land snails mostly eat green plants.

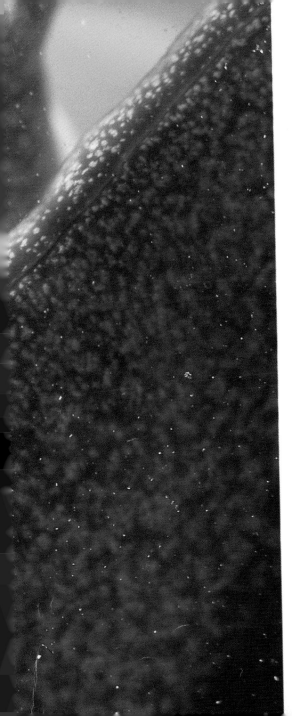

Many sea snails are also plant eaters. But some are predators that dine on other sea animals. The moon snail has a radula that is strong enough to drill through clam shells. This snail bores a hole, and then dines on the soft clam inside. Nudibranchs are also meat-eaters. They hold prey in their teeth, scraping pieces off with their radula.

Inside a snail's mouth is a file-like organ called a radula. The mouth of a mystery snail is pictured here.

13

These West Coast land snails, like all snails, prefer to keep themselves cool and protected from sunlight.

In humid, warm climates, snails and slugs are active all year. In cold climates, they spend winter in a dormant, or inactive, state. Slugs dig into the soil and cover themselves with a winter coat of mucus, so they won't dry out. Snails pull into their shells and close the opening with a mucus barrier. Because land snails and slugs need lots of moisture (for all the mucus they secrete), they do the same thing during dry weather. When warm, moist weather returns, the animals wake up and start moving around.

Even in moist weather, slugs and snails shun sunlight, which could dry them out. They spend sunny days under rocks, leaves, and logs, and come out at night and in cloudy weather.

Land snails and slugs are especially unusual in one respect. They are hermaphrodites. This means that they have both male and female characteristics. When they mate, they actually exchange sperm. Then each snail (or slug) lays a cluster of eggs, usually in a shady, damp place. Water snails are generally male or female. Only the male has sperm, and only the female lays eggs. The eggs are laid in the water, protected by a pouch or a mass of jelly.

Top: **A land snail laying eggs**
Bottom: **A slug laying eggs**

Slug and snail eggs hatch only weeks after being laid. Here, land snail eggs begin to hatch.

The adults don't stay to guard the eggs, which hatch in a few weeks. Newborn snails and slugs are fully independent, miniature versions of adults. They are ready to find food and start living on their own. Depending on the species, they reach adulthood and are ready to mate when they are anywhere from a few months to two years old. Some snail and slug species live as long as twenty years, while others live just a year or two. And many become food for other animals. Ducks, geese, snakes, toads, turtles, crabs, and certain fish are among the animals that like to dine on slugs and snails.

A box turtle prepares to snap up a slug.

SNAILS, SLUGS, AND PEOPLE

In many parts of the world, snails are food for people. Fine French restaurants are famous for serving up escargots, snails roasted in butter and garlic. Snail "farms" raise many edible varieties. Sometimes even slugs end up on the dinner table.

Snails and slugs can also be plant pests, and in some places they cause serious problems. The brown garden snail is a common pest in California. People first brought these snails there in the 1850s, as a food source. In Vietnam, the South American golden snail has caused great damage. These snails were introduced in Vietnam in the late 1980s, in the hope that they would become an important export crop. Instead, the snails quickly spread through Vietnamese rice paddies. They now devour thousands of acres of rice plants and other crops each year.

Chemicals that kill snails also kill fish and other animals. For that reason, people usually try to control snails and slugs without chemicals. Slugs and snails can be hand-picked from plants or captured in baited traps. It is also good to clear away debris where these animals may shelter. Gardeners often keep snails and slugs off plants with barriers of copper flashing, which reacts with snail slime. A three-inch- (8-centimeter-) wide barrier of ashes will also stop them—slugs and snails can't secrete enough slime to glide through the powdery material.

SLUG-FEST USA

Maybe it's the slime. Maybe it's the size. For whatever reason, the banana slug has won a special place in American culture. These slugs live in the damp redwood forests of the Pacific Northwest. They're yellowish, with black spots like a ripe banana. They're about as big as bananas, too. They grow up to 10 inches (25 centimeters) long and can weigh a quarter pound (1 gram). Some towns in coastal northern California hold annual banana slug festivals, with special activities (and recipes) featuring the slugs. And the banana slug is the official mascot of the University of California at Santa Cruz!

Slugs and snails that eat plants can be pests to humans.

Only a few of the thousands of kinds of snails and slugs cause problems for people. The rest just go slowly about their business, silently filling their important place in the natural world.

2

Collecting and Caring for Snails and Slugs

On the following pages, you'll find instructions for collecting and keeping freshwater and land snails and slugs. These animals are easy to find and to care for. (Snails can also be bought from aquarium stores and biological supply companies.) Sea snails and nudibranchs have special needs that make them very difficult to keep, so it's best not to collect them.

You can learn a great deal about snails and slugs just by watching them. Have fun with these little animals, but keep these points in mind:

Snails and slugs need moisture. Without it they become inactive, and eventually they will dry up. When you take snails or slugs out of their container, put them on a moist surface, such as damp paper toweling. Mist them with water from a hand-held spray bottle from time to time. If a snail withdraws into its shell, you can often coax it out by dipping it briefly in water, or setting it on a wet lettuce leaf or other green plant.

Move snails and slugs by picking up the leaves or other plant material they are on, or by coaxing them onto a spoon. You can pick up snails by their shells, but it's best not to pick up soft-bodied slugs with your hands (and you probably won't want to). Don't move or handle slugs or snails more than is necessary. Too much handling is bad for them. Always wash your hands after you're done working with slugs and snails.

If you collect snails or slugs from the wild, release them (in warm weather) back to the place where you found them when you are finished with them. Do not release snails that you buy. They may not be able to live in your area, or they may become pests if they are left to reproduce and inhabit a new area.

What sorts of snails and slugs can you find in the wild? That depends on where you live. In warm weather, you can find snails and slugs of some type almost anywhere in North America that plants grow.

It is always best to transport slugs and snails without touching them directly.

LAND SNAILS AND SLUGS

It is best to search for land snails and slugs in the early morning, on cloudy and misty days, or after a rain. Snail hunting at night, with a flashlight, is also a fun activity. Take along a container with high sides, such as an empty coffee can, to hold your catch. Put some moist (not soggy) soil or leaf litter in the bottom, and punch holes in the lid to let air in.

Look on the undersides of leaves growing near the ground, beneath rocks and fallen branches, under flower pots, and in other damp, sheltered areas. When you find a snail, place it gently into the container. If you find a slug, try to lift it into your container on a leaf or twig.

Old pots, bricks, and pieces of wood often attract snails and slugs seeking moist, shady protection.

CARING FOR LAND SNAILS

As soon as you can, set up a larger and more permanent home for your snails and slugs. You can use a large wide-mouthed glass jar, a small aquarium, or a large plastic food container. Put a few inches of moist (not wet) soil and leaf litter on the bottom. Scatter a few dry leaves, small stones, sticks, or pieces of tree bark on top of the soil to give the animals places to hide. If you can collect some living moss, place that on the soil as well.

Cover the container with vented plastic wrap—the kind sold for keeping vegetables fresh. This will keep snails and moisture in, while letting air circulate. Secure the wrap with a rubber band. You can cover the container with mesh fabric, but it will be harder to keep it moist. If you use regular plastic wrap, you'll need to punch lots of holes in it.

Slug and snail containers should be well ventilated and should provide plenty of room for movement.

Put the container out of direct sunlight and away from heat sources, such as radiators or vents. Mist the interior very lightly with water from a spray bottle. Keep an eye on the moisture level. The soil should be slightly damp, but not soggy. If you see mist or droplets of water collecting on the glass, the environment is too moist. Punch more holes in the cover, and mist less.

Add fresh food to the container each evening. Land snails and slugs are fond of leafy vegetables like spinach and lettuce. They also like fruits and vegetables such as apples, strawberries, carrots, tomatoes, and mushrooms. Provide water by wetting the food first. Snails need calcium for their shells. A good way to provide it is to put clean eggshells or a piece of cuttlebone, which you can get at a pet store, in the container.

Snails and slugs like to eat leafy vegetables but are also fond of carrots, mushrooms, and fruits.

This land snail is crawling across a cuttlebone.

Each day, remove droppings and uneaten food. If you notice that your snails or slugs are inactive, your container may be too dry. To revive them, mist the container well, dip the snails or slugs briefly in water, and return them to the container along with fresh wet lettuce leaves. If they don't revive within a couple of days, they are probably dead and should be removed.

If the snails or slugs are happy in their new home, they may lay some eggs. Look for clusters of whitish, rubbery eggs under stones, sticks, and leaves.

FRESHWATER SNAILS

Look for freshwater snails at quiet ponds and marshes. Try shallow areas with lots of water plants—snails feed on these plants. If you sweep a long-handled collecting net through the water in a weedy spot, you'll probably turn up some snails. You can buy a net, but it's easy to make one.

What to Do:

Tape the food strainer tightly to the mop handle. Or, if you're using a mesh bag, do this:

1. Bend the hanger to form a round loop. Straighten the hanger's hook. (Ask an adult to help if the hanger is hard to bend.)
2. Put your bag through the loop, so that it forms a pouch.
3. At the open end, fold the mesh fabric over the wire loop, and sew it in place.
4. Tape the net to the handle.

Take along a wide-mouthed container to hold your snails. The container must have a cover, because snails can crawl up out of the water. Take just a few snails. Be sure the cover has holes to let in air. Fill it with pond water, and add some pond plants and green algae before you place the snails inside.

You may also find it helpful to bring along a shallow container, such as a plastic dishpan or food keeper. Empty your net into the flat pan first, and sort out the snails and plants you want. Put those in your collecting jar, and return the rest of the material to the pond.

When you visit a pond or marsh, take an adult with you. Follow these steps for safety:

Wear old sneakers or sandals for wading. Don't go barefoot—glass or sharp stones may be hidden under the water.

Use your net handle or another pole to test the depth of the water ahead as you wade to be sure that the bottom doesn't drop off suddenly.

Don't search in streams with fast currents. They can be dangerous, and you'll find few snails there.

Don't hunt for snails from a boat or a dock where you might fall in deep water.

CARING FOR FRESHWATER SNAILS

When you get your snails home, put them in a large wide-mouthed jar or an aquarium filled with water. Use pond water or spring water if you can. Most tap water contains chlorine, which may be harmful to the snails. You can use tap water if you first let it stand for 24 hours. This allows the chlorine to evaporate out of the water. Or you can treat tap water with chlorine remover, which is available at pet stores. The water should be at room temperature before you put in the snails.

Put pond plants and algae in the container along with the snails. Cover it with screening or mesh fabric, secured with a rubber band, so the snails won't crawl out. Place the container away from heat sources. The plants will need bright light for a couple of hours every day to stay healthy. But don't leave the container in the sun, or the water will become too warm for the snails.

Keep your water snail home out of direct sunlight so it does not become too warm.

Egg clusters look like blobs of jelly with tiny dots or balls inside.

The snails will eat the pond plants, and you'll need to add more plants frequently. You can also feed the snails lettuce and spinach. Boil the leaves briefly before you put them in the water. Remove droppings and uneaten food daily. If the water smells bad or turns cloudy, set up a new container. Transfer living snails and plants, and discard the dead ones.

Snails may lay eggs in their new home. Look for egg masses on plant leaves or the sides of the container. The clusters look like blobs of jelly with lots of tiny dots. When the eggs hatch, each dot will be a snail.

3

Investigating Snails and Slugs

Keeping slugs and snails gives you a chance to watch them up close. On the following pages, you'll find activities and experiments that will help you learn more about them. Some of these activities are designed for freshwater snails, and some for land snails or slugs. Animals collected from the wild should always be returned to the place where they were found when you have finished studying them.

WHAT DO LAND SNAILS AND SLUGS LIKE TO EAT?

Do snails and slugs have favorite foods? Are they picky eaters, or will they nibble on anything? Before you begin this activity, make a prediction based on what you already know about snails and slugs. Then follow the steps on the next page to see if your prediction is correct.

What You Need:

* Flat plastic container, such as a shallow food keeper or sandwich box
* Vented plastic wrap and rubber band, to cover the container
* Equal-size pieces of lettuce, apple, carrot, grape, mushroom, or other vegetables
* Several land snails or slugs

What to Do:

1. Put pieces of several different foods in the container. Gently place your snails or slugs inside, and mist lightly.

2. Cover the container with vented plastic wrap, held in place with a rubber band. Put it in a quiet place out of direct sunlight.

3. Check the container after six to eight hours and note which foods were eaten. Then return the animals to their big container.

Results: Which foods did your snails or slugs eat? Repeat this experiment with other foods. (Do not use salted foods. Contact with salt is harmful to snails and slugs.)

Conclusion: What do your results tell you about the foods snails and slugs like to eat?

33

HOW MUCH DO SNAILS AND SLUGS EAT?

Farmers don't like snails and slugs because they eat important crops. But how much can a little snail or slug eat? Make a prediction based on what you know. Then do this activity to find out if you're right.

What You Need:

* Flat plastic container, such as a shallow food keeper or sandwich box
* Vented plastic wrap and rubber band, to cover container
* Graph paper and pencil
* Piece of lettuce
* A land snail or slug

What to Do:

1. Put the lettuce on the graph paper and trace its outline.
2. Put the leaf in the container, gently place your snail or slug on it, and mist lightly.
3. Cover the container with vented plastic wrap, held in place with a rubber band. Put it in a quiet place out of direct sunlight.

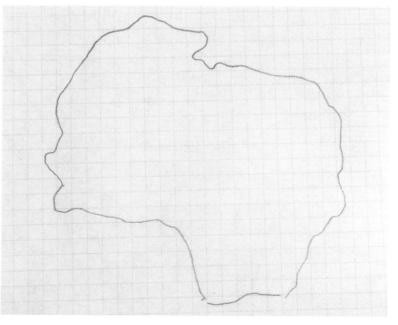

4. Check the container every few hours. If the snail has been eating, put the animal back in its large container.

5. Set the lettuce on the graph paper, over the old outline. Mark any graph squares where lettuce was eaten.

Results: How many "squares" of lettuce did your snail or slug eat? How many were untouched? Try this experiment again, but leave the animal on the lettuce longer. How long does it take to eat the whole leaf? Or use a different animal—a slug instead of a snail, for example. Which eats more?

Conclusion: Based on your results, do you think farmers should be concerned about snails and slugs? Remember that there may be hundreds of these animals in a farmer's field, eating all night long.

CAN FRESHWATER SNAILS CONTROL ALGAE GROWTH?

Algae are simple plants that grow in the water. A common type of algae coats rocks and underwater branches with silky green strands. Sometimes algae grows so thickly that it chokes out other plants and makes it hard for some water animals to live. Algae growth is a problem in aquariums, too. Can snails help? Decide what you think, and then test your answer with this experiment.

What to Do:

1. Place equal amounts of water in the two jars.
2. Put an equal amount of algae-covered stones (or sticks) in each. If the water level is still the same in both containers, you'll know that you've put in equal amounts of stones.
3. Put one or two water snails in one jar. Cover it with mesh, secured with a rubber band, so the snails won't escape. The other jar has no snails, but cover it with mesh, too. That way both jars will be the same.
4. Place the jars side by side in a brightly lit place, but not in direct sunlight.
5. Check the jars over the next few weeks and compare the amount of algae growth.

Results: Which jar has the most algae?
Conclusion: Decide whether a snail would be good to have in an aquarium. Can you think of reasons why, and why not? Try this experiment with different kinds of freshwater snails, to see if some are better at algae-control than others.

What You Need:
* Two small jars, the same size and shape
* Mesh and rubber band, to cover the jars
* Pond water or chlorine-free tap water
* Small algae-covered stones or sticks, collected from the edge of a pond
* One or two freshwater snails

HOW DOES COLD AFFECT THE EGGS OF FRESHWATER SNAILS?

In places with cold winters, water in deep ponds often stays chilly for weeks after warm spring weather arrives. Can a snail's eggs develop and hatch in these cold conditions? Do this activity to find out.

What to Do:

1. Fill the jars with water to the same level.
2. Place an egg mass (along with a piece of the plant to which it's attached) in each jar.
3. Put one container indoors at room temperature. Put the other in a cold place, such as an unheated basement. The containers should be out of direct sunlight, and both should get the same amount of light.
4. Check the containers every day. Use a magnifying glass to see how the eggs change. Make a record of what you see. You can include sketches of the eggs.

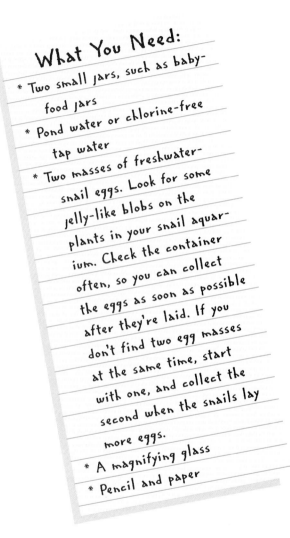

What You Need:
* Two small jars, such as baby-food jars
* Pond water or chlorine-free tap water
* Two masses of freshwater-snail eggs. Look for some jelly-like blobs on the plants in your snail aquarium. Check the container often, so you can collect the eggs as soon as possible after they're laid. If you don't find two egg masses at the same time, start with one, and collect the second when the snails lay more eggs.
* A magnifying glass
* Pencil and paper

Results: Did the eggs in both jars develop at the same rate? Or did the eggs in one jar hatch first? (When the eggs hatch, move the new snails to your snail aquarium.)

Conclusion: What do your results tell you about the affect of cold on snail eggs? Based on what you saw, when do you think snails are most likely to be born?

DO SNAILS PREFER DARK OR LIGHT PLACES?

You can do this activity with freshwater snails, land snails, or slugs. First, make a prediction, based on what you know about these animals.

What to Do:

1. If you are using a freshwater snail, fill the container with chlorine-free water. If you are using a land snail or slug, put an evenly moistened paper towel in the container.
2. Put the container in a well-lit place. Lay the towel over the top so that it covers half the container.
3. Place your snail in the center of the container and watch what it does.

Results: Does the snail move toward or away from the light? Repeat the experiment several times to see if you get the same results.

Conclusion: Was your prediction correct? Try this experiment with a different type of snail. If you used a freshwater snail the first time, try a land snail or a slug.

What You Need:
* A plastic container, such as a shallow food keeper
* A dark towel or other cloth
* A freshwater snail, land snail, or slug

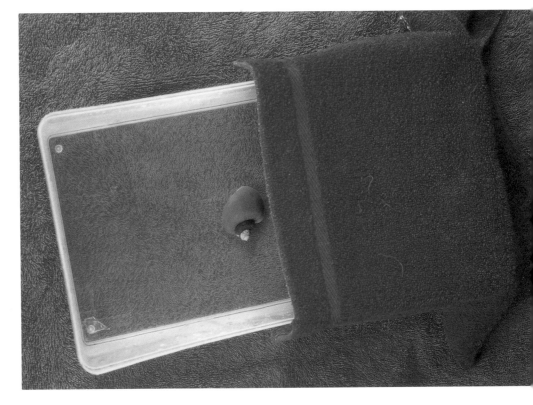

MORE ACTIVITIES WITH SNAILS AND SLUGS

These activities work best with land snails and slugs.

1. Use a magnifying glass for a close-up look at a snail or slug. Find the eyes and the mouth. See if you can locate the animal's breathing hole. Is it always open, or does it close?

2. Put a snail or slug on a damp paper towel. How does it move? Where does the slime come from? What does the animal do when you put an obstacle in its path? When you gently touch its back?

3. Move the snail or slug onto a fresh lettuce leaf, and listen closely. Can you hear the radula moving back and forth as it rasps off bits of lettuce?

4. Find out how fast a snail's pace really is. Draw a circle 12 inches (30.5 centimeters) across on a sheet of paper. Mist the paper with water, and put a snail or slug in the middle of the circle. How long does it take the animal to get to the edge? Have a snail race—compare the speeds of different snails and slugs. If you put a lettuce leaf outside the circle, do the animals go toward it? Do they go faster?

Mark a circle to help you observe how fast a snail moves.

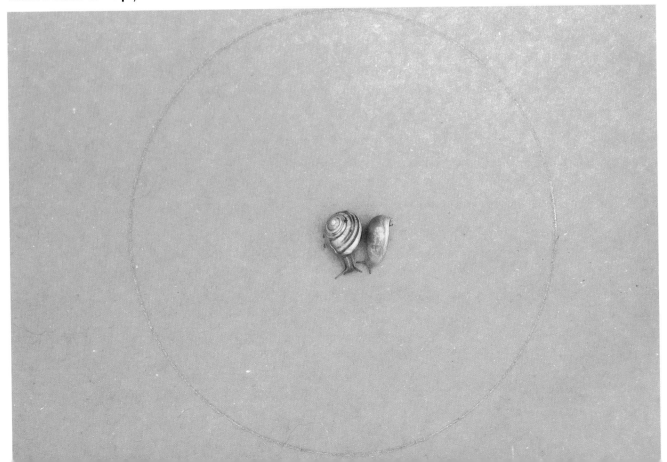

Mark a snail to help you track its movement outdoors.

5. See where snails go outdoors. Find a garden snail, and mark its shell with a dot of nail polish. (This won't hurt the snail.) Note where you found it, and check back in an hour. How far did it travel? Check the area morning and evening over several days. Does the marked snail come back to the same place for food and shelter?

6. Look in your yard for plants that snails and slugs have eaten. Early morning is a good time for this. The animals may still be feeding, and you'll probably find their slime trails. Which leaves and fruits do they prefer?

RESULTS AND CONCLUSIONS

Here are some possible results and conclusions for the activities on pages 33 to 39. When you do these activities, you may not get the same outcomes. Many things affect the way snails and slugs behave. If your results differ, think about what the reasons may be. What conditions might have led to your results? If you can, repeat the activity, and see if the outcome is the same.

What Do Land Snails and Slugs Like to Eat?

Most snails and slugs will head for leafy vegetables first. They're also fond of fruits and berries. But they'll eat almost any plant food—even oatmeal.

Slugs and snails will eat almost any kind of plant.

How Much Do Snails and Slugs Eat?

How much your snail eats will depend mostly on its size. Snails eat steadily, and in large numbers they can do a lot of damage. Farmers in Vietnam have found as many as 200 golden snails per square yard in their fields. Each snail can eat more than a square foot of rice plants in a day!

An adult mystery snail.

Can Snails Control Algae Growth?

Snails eat algae, so you'll probably see less growth in the snail container. Snails will help keep algae in check in aquariums. But even so, many people who keep fish don't want snails—because the snails will eat aquarium plants, too.

How Does Cold Affect the Eggs of Freshwater Snails?

Snail eggs develop more slowly in cold water. In places where winters are cold, late spring and summer are the best times for snails to reproduce.

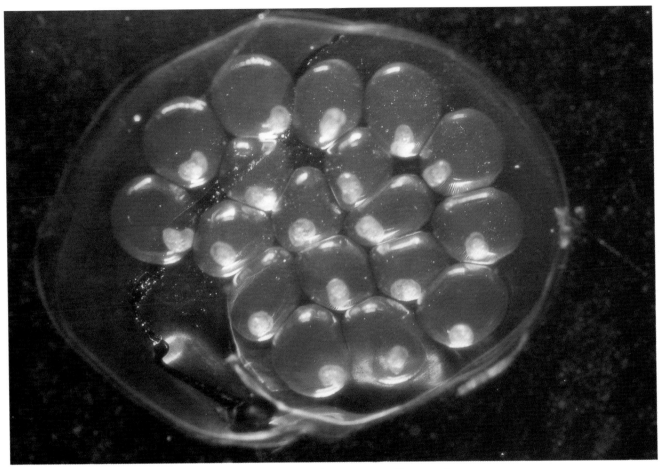

Many individual snails can be seen developing inside this water snail's egg cluster.

Do Snails Prefer Dark or Light Places?

Many freshwater snails don't seem to care whether they are in light or shade. Land snails and slugs try to avoid strong light, however. In nature, constant exposure to sunlight could dry these animals out.

SOME WORDS ABOUT SNAILS AND SLUGS

dormant: Inactive.

hermaphrodite: Having both male and female characteristics.

mantle: A layer of tissue on the back of a snail or slug. The mantle produces the snail's shell.

mollusks: A large group of soft-bodied animals. Mollusks have no skeletons; most, but not all, have shells.

mucus: A thick, moist, slippery substance produced by slugs and snails.

radula: A rough, tonguelike mouthpart that snails use to saw off bits of food.

terrestrial: Living on land.

SOURCES FOR SNAILS

These companies sell live snails and other materials through the mail. If you buy snails through mail-order sources such as these, do not release them into the wild.

Carolina Biological Supply
2700 York Road
Burlington, NC 27215
1-800-334-5551

Connecticut Valley Biological
82 Valley Road, P.O. Box 326
Southampton, MA 01073
1-800-628-7748

FOR FURTHER READING

Buholzer, Theresa. *Life of the Snail*. Minneapolis, MN: Carolrhoda, 1987.

Coldrey, Jennifer. *Discovering Snails and Slugs*. Charlottesville, VA: Bookwright Press, 1987.

Fisher, Enid. *Snails*. Milwaukee, WI: Gareth Stevens, 1996.

Henwood, Chris. *Snails and Slugs*. Danbury, CT: Franklin Watts, 1988.

Ross, Michael Elshon. *Snailology*. Minneapolis, MN: Lerner, 1996.

Stone, Lynn M. *Snails and Slugs*. Vero Beach, FL: Rourke, 1995.

INDEX

Note: Page numbers in italics indicate pictures

Algae, 36

Banana slug, 18
Brains, 10
Breathing, 6, 9
Brown garden snail, 18

Cone snails, 11

Cowries, 8

Eggs and Egg-laying, *15–17*, 27, 30, *31*, *45*
Experiments (with snails and slugs)
  algae control, *36*
  body parts, 40

cold temperatures and eggs, *37–38*
favorite foods, *32–33*
light preferences, *39*
listening to radula, 41
movement, 40
outdoor food preferences, 42

outdoor tracking, *42*
quantity of food, *34–35*
results and conclusions,
   43–45
speed, *41*
Eyes, *9*

Foot, 8

Gastropod, 8

Mantle, 8, 9
Mating, 15, 16
Mollusks, 6, 7
Mouth, 9, *12–13*
Mystery snail, *6, 12–13, 44*

Nudibranchs, 4, 6, 13, 20

Olive snails, 8
Operculum, 8

Periwinkle, *6*
Poison. *See* Venom

Radula, 11, *13*
Ramshorn water snail, *6*

Safety measures, 29
Sea slugs. *See* Nudibranchs
Sea snails, *6, 7, 8, 9, 12–13,*
   20
Shells, *7, 8,* 26
Slime (mucus), 8, 14, 18
Slugs
   climate for, 4, 14, 22
   collecting, *20–31*
   conditions for, 24
   containers for, 25, 26
   as food, 4, 18
   food of, 4, 11, 13, *26, 43*
   habitat of, 4, 6, 18, 24
   and humans, 18–19
   kinds of, 4, 6
   life span of, 17
   movement of, 8
   predators of, *17*
   protection against, 18
   size of, 4, 18
   transporting, 22, 23, 24

Snails
   climate for, 4, 14, 22
   collecting, *20–31*
   conditions for, 24
   containers for, 25, 26, *30*
   as food, 4
   food of, 4, *11,* 13, 18,
      19, 26, 27, 28, 31, *43*
   growth of, 8
   habitat of, 4, 6, 24
   and humans, 18–19
   kinds of, 6
   life span of, 17
   movement of, 8
   predators of, 17
   protection against, 18
   size of, 4
   and temperature, *14*
   transporting, 22, *23,* 24
   *See also specific snail
      names*

Tentacles, *9, 10*

Venom, 11

48